D1070845

Victorians Abroad

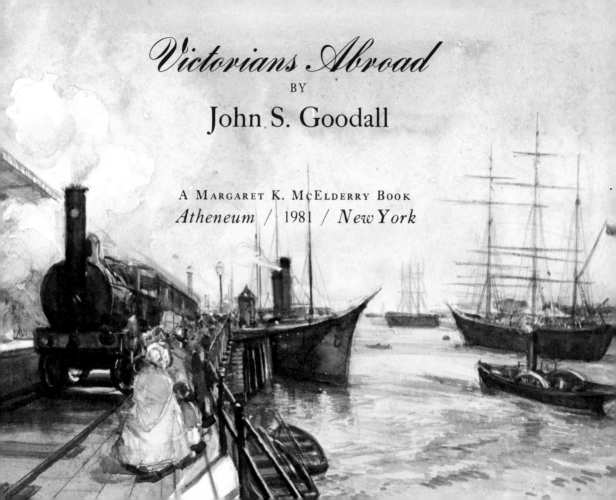

Victorians Abroad

BY

John S. Goodall

A MARGARET K. McELDERRY BOOK

Atheneum / 1981 / New York

Library of Congress catalog card number: 80-67431
ISBN 0-689-50191-9
Printed in Hong Kong
First American Edition

Note

This book shows the English traveling abroad at various times during Queen Victoria's long reign (1837–1901). The first pages depict the Grand Tour in the 1840s and the last ones a voyage to India in the 1890s. The order of the pictures and the subjects they represent are as follows:

Departure from England (title-page); Customs; French café; Switzerland; Crossing the Alps; Venice; Florence, the Uffizi Gallery; Rome; Pompeii; Biarritz; Paris, shopping; Versailles; Paris, Closerie des Lilas; Montmarte; Nice, Avenue Masséna; Monte Carlo; Deauville; Evian, taking the waters; Dresden, finishing school; Egypt, the Pyramids; Egypt, the Nile; Africa, exploration; Ship to India; Disembarking at Bombay; The Gymkhana Club; Calcutta, Viceregal Garden Party; Kashmir, the Dal Lake; Camping in the Kulu Valley; Simla; Malta, barn dance on a battleship; Dover.

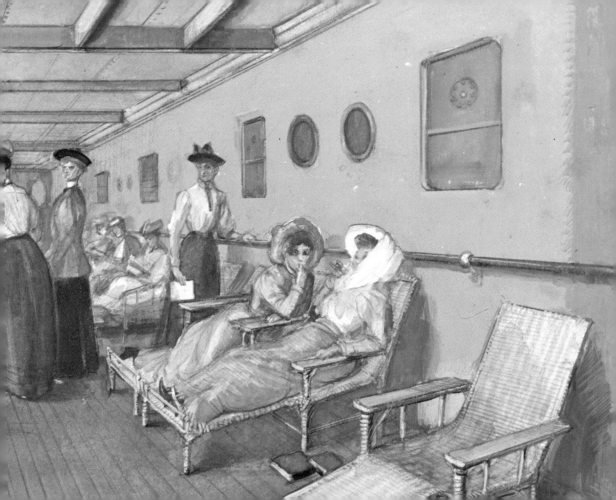